Scrubs & More

Designs by Lorine Mason

HOUSE of WHITE BIRCHES

PUBLISHERS
SINCE 1947

Introduction

Drab is out, and personal style is the name of the game these days, even for scrubs, the loose-fitting, functional clothes worn in a "scrubbed" environment. Not just for medical personnel anymore, the casual and comfortable nature of scrubs translates well to loungewear as scrubs can be found in use at spas, retreats and clinics of all types.

This book contains scrubs and scrubs embellishments with trendy good looks to fit your profession, lifestyle and mood. With the combinations of color, pattern and clever embellishing techniques found in this book, ordinary scrubs will become unique enough to satisfy even the most fashion-conscious professional. Scrubs with a touch of fashion still need to remain totally functional. This is possible through the use of easy-care fabrics and simple construction techniques, which work together to allow the freedom of movement and comfort desired by professionals of all types.

The tips and techniques in this book will allow you to embellish plain scrubs in order to give yourself something unique to wear.

Meet The Designer

Lorine Mason is an author, project designer and regular columnist whose work has been featured in print, on the Web and television. She works with a variety of art mediums, combining them with her enthusiasm for all things fabric. She strives to create items others will be inspired to re-create, hopefully adding their own personal touches. Her creative career started in retail, weaving its way through management and education positions along the path. This experience, along with a goal to stay on top of trends in color and style, gives her current work the edge manufacturers, publishers and editors have come to expect. She shares her life with husband, Bill, and daughters, Jocelyn and Kimbrely. They currently live in Virginia, having moved there from Winnipeg, Manitoba, by way of Beaconsfield, Quebec.

Table of Contents

Summer Silhouettes,
page 26

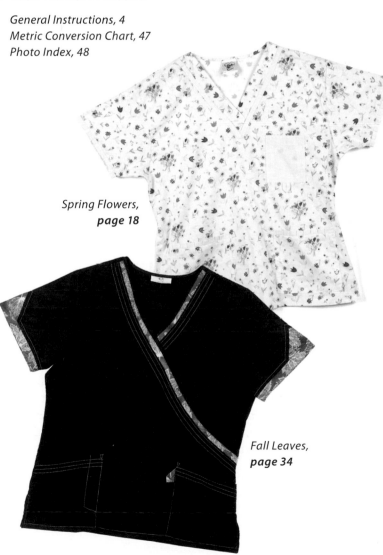

Spring Flowers,
page 18

Fall Leaves,
page 34

House of White Birches, Berne, Indiana 46711   Clotilde.com

General Instructions

By Lorine Mason

Ready-Made or Homemade Scrubs

Starting with a quality pair of scrubs is a must. Your time is too precious to waste on inferior-quality garments. A garment is, frankly, not worth your time unless the garment and the intended embellishments will stand up to your professional requirements.

Scrubs, by nature, are meant to be durable. So, whether you choose to purchase ready-made scrubs and deconstruct them to add your personal touch, or start from scratch, the quality of the fabric and embellishments should remain your highest priority.

Most of the techniques shown in this book were used on ready-made scrubs, but can be transferred to scrubs you might make yourself, i.e. the scrub top for Wintergreen Stripes. Take a few moments to look over the instructions of a project, and then adapt them to the construction of your scrubs.

If you want to make your own scrubs, I recommend Kwik-Sew Patterns #2807, #3201, #3708 and #3709. These patterns are a great base for the embellishment techniques in this book.

Basic Sewing Supplies & Equipment

Seam Rippers

A good seam ripper is imperative to success when deconstructing garments. I personally like one with an ergonomic handle and a fairly long blade, but there are many styles from which to choose. Try some of the different styles and choose the one that best fits your hand.

Make sure the blade is sharp and free of nicks, which can cause pulls and tears in the fabric. The blade should also have a sharp tip which will allow you to pick up and cut threads more easily.

Fusible Web Tape & Fabric

When attaching an appliqué or piece of trim to a garment, you will sometimes need an extra hand. Steam-A-Seam 2 is perfect for the many projects that need that an "extra-hand."

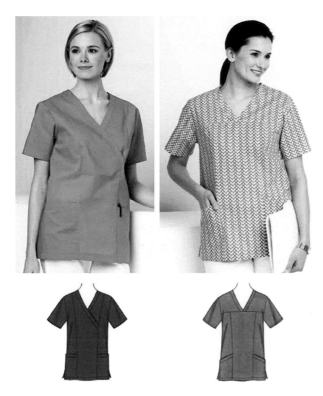

This fusible web comes in the following two varieties: ¼-inch-wide and ½-inch-wide tape, and fabric that is available by the yard or in packages of 9 x 12-inch sheets. Using a fusible web to back decorative fabric deters fraying and gives the opportunity for all kinds of appliqué shapes and sizes. Follow the manufacturer's instructions for beautiful appliqués without stitching.

Gel Roller Fabric Pen

I absolutely love the gel roller fabric pen. It gives even beginner artists the capability to doodle directly onto the fabric with an ink that flows consistently, leaving clean lines. You can go back over areas, filling in around curves for a more dramatic look or adding details like shading. Heat setting assures a permanent design on natural fabrics (as well as a number of synthetics I have tried). Test the pen on a scrap of fabric prior to decorating your garment. Follow the manufacturer's instructions for heat-setting the ink.

In addition to the above, the following standard sewing notions should be on hand:

- Scissors of various sizes, including pinking shears
- Rotary cutter(s), mats and straightedges
- Pattern tracing paper or cloth
- Pressing tools such as sleeve rolls and pressing boards
- Pressing equipment, including ironing board and iron; press cloths
- Straight pins and pincushion

- Measuring tools
- Marking pens (either air- or water-soluble) or tailor's chalk
- Spray adhesive (temporary)
- Seam sealant
- Hand-sewing needles and thimble
- Point turners
- Large-eye needle

Basic Tips & Techniques

Deconstructing a Garment

In these projects, I took ready-made garments and opened the seams to add embellishments. Follow these simple techniques and deconstruction will be a snap.

Press garment seams flat prior to opening seams. I have found the seam ripper glides more easily along a freshly pressed line of stitching.

When partially opening a seam, place a straight pin at the end of the opening through the seam line to prevent additional unraveling or tearing of the seam.

Measure seam-allowance widths used on ready-made garments. Seam allowances differ and need to be taken into consideration when adding gussets, pockets, plackets, etc. The pattern pieces drafted for this book have ½-inch seam allowances. Simply increase or decrease pattern seam allowances to correspond with the garment.

House of White Birches, Berne, Indiana 46711   Clotilde.com

Bias Strips

To cut bias strips, fold fabric diagonally so crosswise grain straight edge is parallel to selvage or lengthwise grain. Cut fabric along this fold line to mark the true bias (Figure 1).

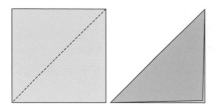

Figure 1

Using a clear ruler, mark successive bias lines the width of the bias strip desired. Carefully cut along line. Handle edges carefully to avoid stretching (Figure 2).

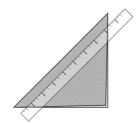

Figure 2

Pin individual bias strips perpendicular to each other with raw edges aligned and right sides together. Sew a diagonal seam to join strips in a continuous strip. Trim seams to ¼ inch and press open (Figure 3).

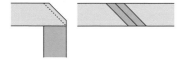

Figure 3

Fold strip in half lengthwise, wrong sides together. Press. Open with wrong side up. Fold each edge to center fold and press. Fold in half again and press (Figure 4).

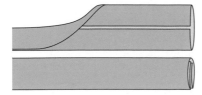

Figure 4

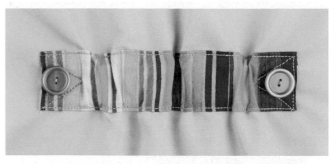

Inserting Elastic Into Casings

Attach a safety pin (or turning tool) to one end of the elastic length. Feed the safety pin through the casing, pulling the elastic into the casing until the elastic-length end is just inside the casing end.

Secure the elastic with a straight pin. Continue pulling the elastic through the casing. Secure the elastic with a straight pin close to the casing end. Remove the safety pin.

While holding the elastic in place, remove straight pin and carefully release elastic to just inside the casing end. Re-pin to secure.

When stitching casing ends closed, stitch through elastic to hold in place.

Creating a Looped Tab

Several of the garments in this book use looped tabs inserted in pockets or gussets.

Using the width and length of fabric suggested in the project instructions, fold the fabric in half lengthwise, with right sides together, and stitch using a ½-inch seam. Turn right side out and press. Cut the required length and mark center of length. Referring to Figure 5, fold fabric length to make tab.

Figure 5

Transferring a Design Pattern

The easiest way to transfer a design pattern to a garment is with fabric transfer paper. Layer the garment, right side up; transfer paper, colored side down; and a copy of the design. Use low-tack tape or straight pins to hold the layers in place.

Trace over the design using a stylus or a retracted ballpoint pen. For large simple designs, you could create a cardboard template of the design and trace around the edges with a water-soluble fabric marker. Or simply sketch the design directly on the garment with a water-soluble fabric marker.

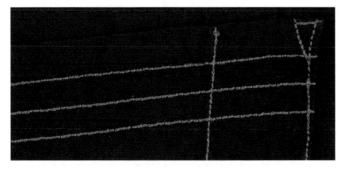

Topstitching & Decorative Stitches

Topstitching is done on the right side of the garment. All topstitching is done in a complementary color to the garment, unless noted otherwise in the project instructions.

Even a simple decorative stitch can add strength and a punch of color to any garment. Since scrubs need to be durable, I chose a durable stitch for all decorative stitching on these projects—the saddle stitch. The saddle stitch is a triple straight stitch found on most sewing machines. It is a durable, yet simple, stitch that is a subtle complement to the embellishments found in this book.

You could also use a complementary color of buttonhole twist thread and a single straight stitch to achieve a similar look. Or you can choose another decorative stitch from your machine's available stitches.

Finishing Seams

Finishing interior seams gives a garment a professional look and strengthens those seams. Use an overcast or combination straight/zigzag stitch found on most sewing machines to stitch the seam allowances together. Stitch in a coordinating thread color. Press the finished seam to the back of the garment. ❖

Sources: *Memory Craft 6600 sewing machine from Janome America Inc.; Kwik-Sew patterns #2807, #3201, #3708 and #3709 from Kwik-Sew Pattern Co. Inc.; Gel Roller for Fabric pen from Pentel of America Ltd.; Steam-a-Seam 2 fusible web from The Warm Company; Knot Us ready-made scrub tops and pants from Simply Basic.*

Wintergreen Stripes

Mixing blue and green has been popular for years. Use a wonderful striped fabric to add a pop of color, and you have a sure winner. Opt for random falls of color or take time to mirror the stripe patterns when adding the embellishment fabric to the scrubs top's symmetrical princess seams and pockets.

Materials
- Kwik-Sew Pattern #3708 in your size
- Lime green fabric as indicated on pattern
- Purchased royal blue elastic-waist scrubs pants in your size
- ¾ yard striped fabric
- 3 (½-inch) lime green buttons
- 2 (¾-inch) royal blue buttons
- ¼ yard 1-inch-wide elastic
- Blue gel roller fabric pen
- Basic sewing supplies and equipment

Scrubs Top

Cutting
From lime green fabric:
- Following directions for View B of Kwik-Sew Pattern #3708, lay out and cut all pattern pieces except front and back neckband and back casing.

From striped fabric:
- Cut four 1 x 45-inch strips.
- Cut three 1½ x 45-inch strips.
- Cut one back casing using pattern piece from Kwik-Sew Pattern #3708.
- Cut one 5½-piece elastic

Assembly
Notes: *Refer to Kwik-Sew Pattern #3708 for seam allowances and general construction instructions unless otherwise indicated. Use thread to match scrubs top fabric for all stitching.*

1. Fold top hem on each pocket to wrong side as indicated on pattern. Press. Fold ¼ inch to wrong side on both lengthwise edges of each 1½ x 45-inch strip. Cut one 1½-inch strip in half. Pin one piece to pocket right side, 1 inch from top of pocket (Figure 1).

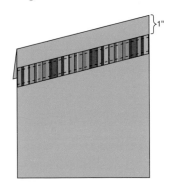

Figure 1

2. Topstitch ⅛ inch from both folded edges of strip, again referring to Figure 1. Pin pockets to front side panels as indicated on pattern. Baste close to pocket sides and bottom. Repeat steps 1 and 2 for second pocket.

3. Press each 1 x 45-inch strip in half lengthwise, wrong sides together. With right sides together, pin and baste 1-inch folded strips to each side of center front panel, matching raw edges. Stitch front side panels to front center panel following pattern instructions. Finish seams with overcast stitch. Press seam allowances toward center panel. Topstitch on either side of seams (Figure 2).

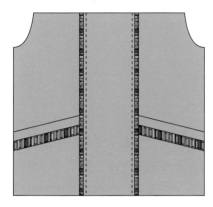

Figure 2

4. Turn ¼ inch to wrong side of back casing on all sides and press. With wrong side of casing to right side of scrubs top, position casing on back where indicated on pattern. Edgestitch casing top and bottom edges.

5. Thread elastic through casing, referring to Inserting Elastic Into Casings on page 6. Stitching through all layers, topstitch close to casing edges and in a triangular shape (Figure 3). Sew one ¾-inch royal blue button to each end of the back waist casing centered over the triangles.

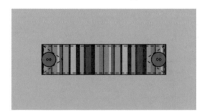

Figure 3

6. With right sides together, stitch front yokes to back at shoulder seams. Finish seams with overcast stitch. Press toward back.

7. Open 1-inch strip flat, wrong side up. Turn ¼ inch of one lengthwise edge toward center fold and press (Figure 4).

Figure 4

8. With right side of strip to wrong side of neckline edge, stitch unfolded edge of strip to neckline using a ¼-inch seam (Figure 5). Press strip away from neckline.

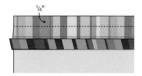

Figure 5

9. Fold strip over seam and pin to front of neckline. Edgestitch strip to neckline (Figure 6).

Figure 6

10. Matching raw edges, pin and baste a 1-inch folded strip to right side of constructed top front at yoke seam. Stitch constructed top front to front yoke following pattern instructions. Finish seam with overcast stitch. Press seam toward scrubs top front. Topstitch on either side of seam.

11. With right sides together and raw edges matching, pin and stitch a 1½-inch strip along the ¼-inch fold line to the bottom edge of either sleeve (Figure 7). Press strip away from sleeve, and then press strip to wrong side of sleeve. Edgestitch folded edge of strip (Figure 8). Repeat steps 10 and 11 for second sleeve.

Figure 7

Figure 8

House of White Birches, Berne, Indiana 46711   Clotilde.com

12. Following pattern instructions, apply sleeves to scrubs top and stitch front to back at side seams. Finish seams with overcast stitch. Press side seams toward garment back. Topstitch to secure in place.

13. Press side slit seam allowances in half to wrong side. Fold again along raw edges and press to make double fold hems. Edgestitch at second fold and across top of slits (Figure 9).

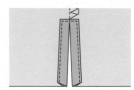

Figure 9

14. Along bottom edge, turn ½ inch to wrong side and press. Fold again ½ inch to wrong side and press, creating a ½-inch double-fold hem. Stitch close to first fold (Figure 10).

½"

Figure 10

15. Referring to Transferring a Design Pattern on page 7, transfer the stethoscope template to the scrubs top above left-hand pocket (Figure 11). Using the gel roller fabric pen, trace transferred template lines. Heat-set following manufacturer's instructions.

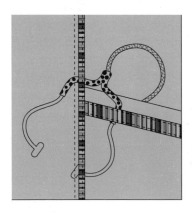

Figure 11

Scrubs Pant

Preparing Garment

1. Remove pants legs hem stitching.

2. Open inner leg seams up to thighs and side leg seams of pants to waistband. Place pins in seams at waistband to anchor seams referring to Deconstructing a Garment on page 5.

3. Open front pocket edges. Secure seams at waistband with pins.

4. Remove cut threads from all seams. Gently press seams flat.

Cutting

From striped fabric:
- Cut three 1½ x 45-inch strips.
- Cut one each pocket A and B.

Assembly

Note: Stitch in original seam allowances unless otherwise indicated.

Pants Pockets

1. Turn ½ inch to wrong side of one short end of each 1½ x 45-inch strip and press. Press each strip in half lengthwise, wrong sides together.

2. Insert one strip between front pocket seams, aligning folded short edge with bottom of waistband. Keeping back pocket out of the way, topstitch through all layers using a decorative stitch (Figure 12). Trim strip even with pocket edge. Set aside remainder of strip. Press pocket edge. Pin pocket to front pants leg.

Figure 12

3. Cut short end of remaining part of strip straight across. Turn ½ inch to wrong side of short end, press. Repeat step 2 for second pants pocket.

Pants Leg Side Seams

1. Pin a 1½ x 45-inch pressed strip to front side seam, aligning folded short end with bottom of waistband and raw edges even. Baste ¼ inch from raw edges. With front and back side seams right sides together, re-stitch original seam depth. Finish seams with overcast stitch. Press seams toward back pants leg. Topstitch on either side of seam, referring Figure 2. Repeat for second pants leg.

2. Lay leg open right side up. Mark 9 inches up from pants leg bottom. Mark a diagonal line from 9-inch mark to edge of back inner leg seam (Figure 13). Mark a second diagonal line 2 inches from the first on the leg front only, again referring to Figure 13 and project photo. Topstitch on lines marked. Repeat for second leg.

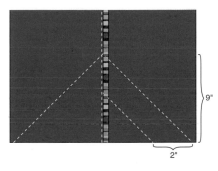

9"

2"

Figure 13

Right-Leg Pockets

1. Fold pocket A and pocket B ¼ inch to wrong side at top and ½ inch on remaining three sides. Press. Fold again on indicated fold line to wrong side at top of pockets and press. Edgestitch on first fold line at top. Topstitch ⅛ inch from top fold.

2. Pin wrong side of pocket B to right side of pocket A, matching placement marks (X, O, Δ). Stitch B to A ⅛ inch from B side edges between squares and triangles (Figure 14).

Figure 14

3. On right leg side seam, mark 19 inches from top of waistband. Pin top of pocket A at mark, centered on seam line.

4. Fold pocket B up out of stitching area. Topstitch side and bottom edges of pocket A (Figure 15a). Fold pocket B down and topstitch from square to triangle around pocket B bottom (Figure 15b). Stitch along pencil pocket sewing line on pocket A. Sew ½-inch lime green buttons where indicated on pocket patterns.

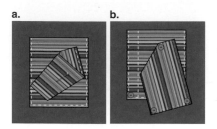

Figure 15

5. With right sides together, re-stitch inner leg seam using thread to match pants. Turn pants right side out. Turn original leg hem allowances to wrong sides and press. Stitch in place using thread to match pants. ❖

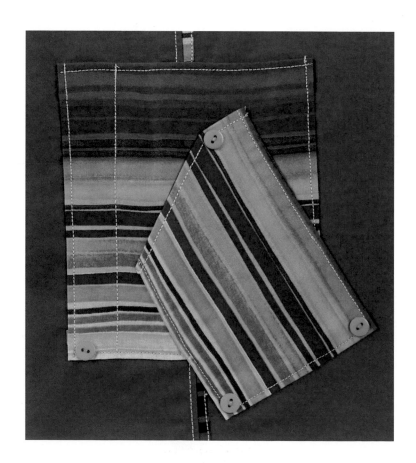

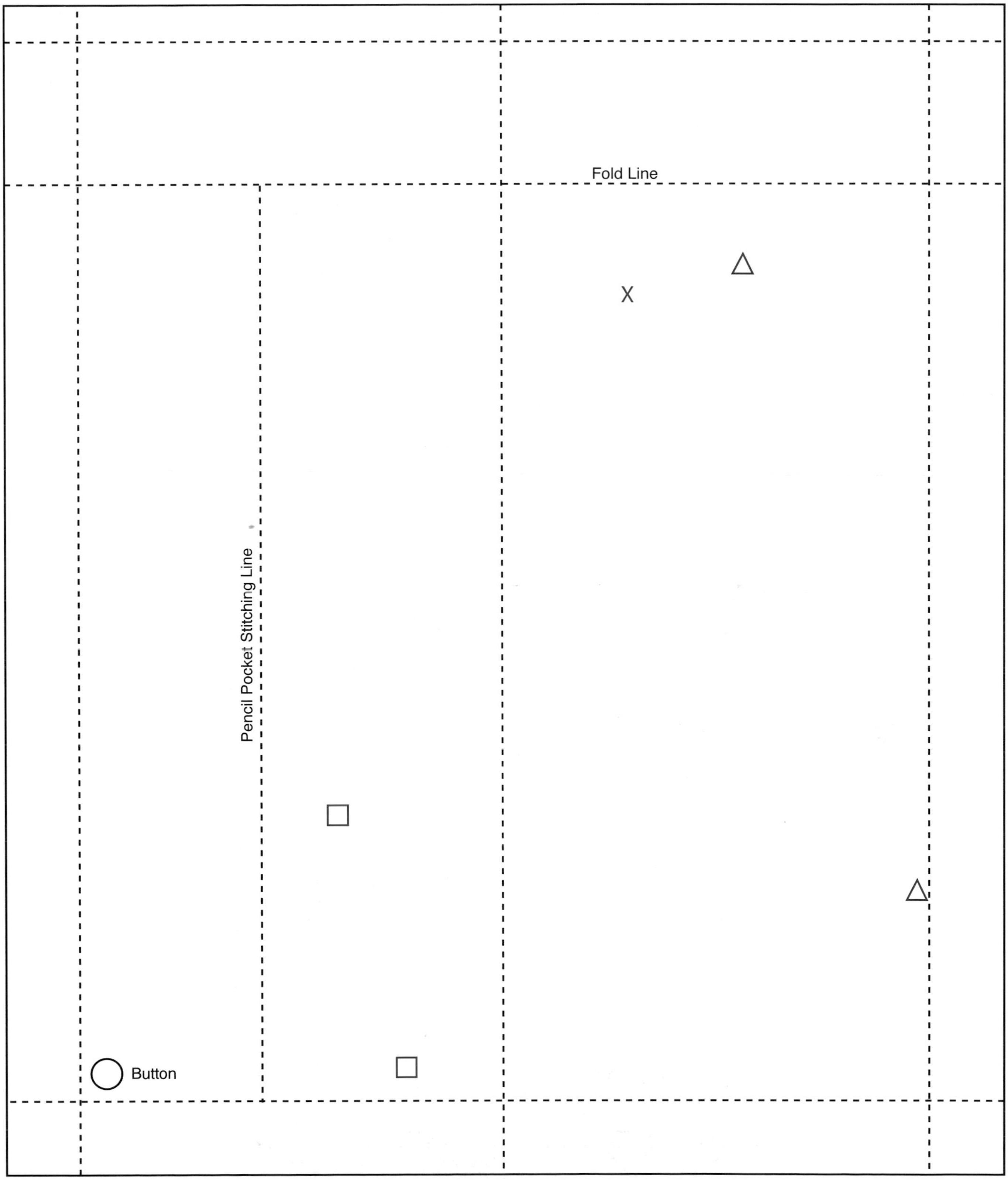

Fold Line

Pencil Pocket Stitching Line

X

△

△

□

□

◯ Button

Wintergreen Stripes
Pocket A
Actual Size

House of White Birches, Berne, Indiana 46711   Clotilde.com

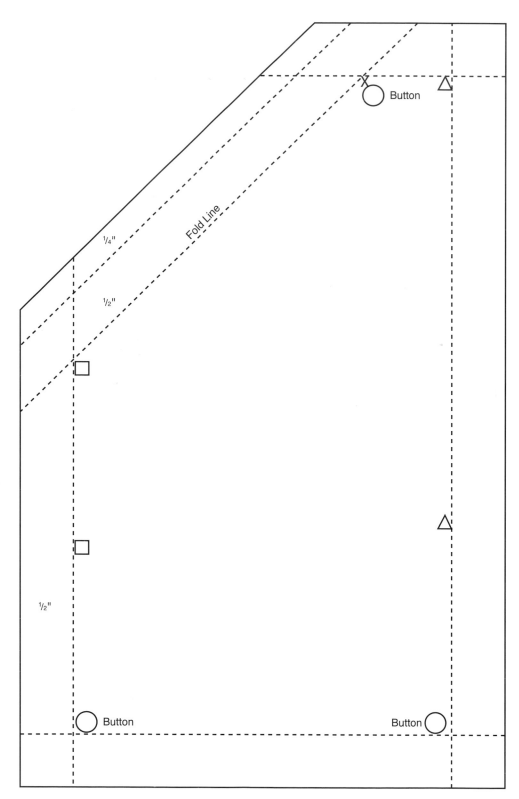

Wintergreen Stripes
Pocket B
Actual Size

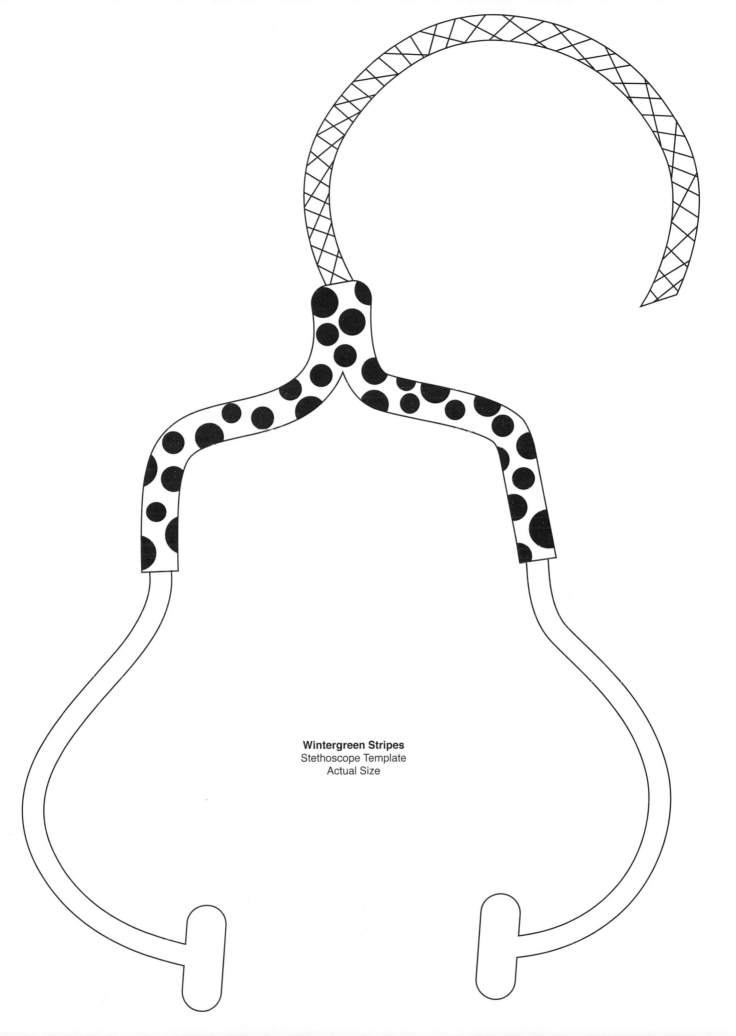

Wintergreen Stripes
Stethoscope Template
Actual Size

Spring Flowers

Step-by-step techniques help you create a personalized scrubs top with creative accents, like a clever drawstring back tie that adds shape without taking away wearing ease. And taking cues from the fanciful prints used for scrubs tops, you can create fun appliqués to embellish the legs of coordinating scrubs pants.

Materials

- Flower-print scrubs top and color-coordinating scrubs pant in your size
- Coordinating assorted fabric scraps in pink, blue, green and yellow
- ½ yard yellow gingham fabric
- Black gel roller fabric pen
- Fusible web
- Basic sewing supplies and equipment

Scrubs Top

Preparing Garment

1. Place a pin 4 inches from the neckline edge of the shoulder seam to anchor the seam, referring to Deconstructing a Garment on page 5. Open the shoulder seams to the pin.

2. Along both side seams, measure 4 inches below the armhole and 4 inches above the hemline. Placing pins at each point to anchor the seams, open both side seams between the pins.

3. Place pins 4 inches down from the top of the hip pockets on both side seams to anchor seams. Open pocket side seams to pins.

4. Remove cut threads from all seams. Gently press seam allowances flat.

Cutting

From yellow gingham fabric:
- Cut one 1 x 45-inch strip for V-neck binding.
- Cut one 1¾ x 45-inch strip for back waistline casing.
- Cut one 1 x 45-inch strip for drawstring.
- Cut one 5½ x 6⅞-inch rectangle for upper pocket.
- Cut three 2 x 45-inch strips for pleated ruffles.

Assembly

V-Neck Binding

1. Press under ¼ inch along both long sides of the 1-inch-wide V-neck binding strip.

2. Lay the strip next to the original neck binding and pin in place. Fold the binding at the peak of the V (Figure 1), and continue pinning the binding strip to the opposite side of the neckline.

Figure 1

3. Edgestitch along folded edges of the binding. Trim the ends of the strip even with shoulder seam allowances.

4. Re-stitch the shoulder seams and finish seam with an overcast stitch.

Back Waistline Casing & Drawstring

1. Have the intended wearer try the scrubs top on. Mark the wearer's natural waistline and the center back (Figure 2).

Center Back

Natural Waistline

Figure 2

2. Press under ¼ inch along both long sides of the 1¾-inch waistline casing strip. Cut the strip in half and turn under one short end of each strip ½ inch. Press.

3. Center the strip over the marked waistline with folded short ends at center back, again referring to Figure 2. Pin in place.

4. Edgestitch top and bottom edges of waistline casing. Trim casing even with side seams.

5. With right sides together, press the 1-inch drawstring strip in half lengthwise. Stitch a lengthwise ¼-inch seam and turn right side out.

6. Cut a 4-inch piece from drawstring and set aside for later use. Cut the remainder of the strip in half. Tie a knot at one end of each piece.

7. Beginning at the center back and using the unknotted end, thread a drawstring piece through one casing (Figure 3), referring to Inserting Elastic Into Casings, page 6. Pin the unknotted end even with the garment edge. Repeat for second drawstring.

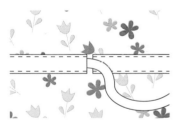

Figure 3

8. Re-stitch the side seams. Finish seams with an overcast stitch.

Upper Pocket

1. Turn under the top edge of the chest pocket ¼ inch along the 5½-inch edge. Fold again 1 inch from the first fold. Press. Edgestitch the top edge of the pocket close to first fold.

2. Turn under, and press ¼ inch along the sides and bottom edges of the pocket. Turn under an additional ⅜ inch along same edges. Press. Pin the hemmed edge of the pocket at the same level as the bottom of the neckline V, centered 8–10 inches below the point where neck and shoulder seams meet (Figure 4). Have the intended wearer try on the scrubs top to check placement.

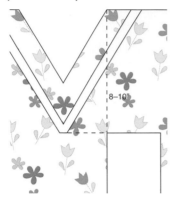

Figure 4

3. Fold 4-inch section of drawstring (set aside earlier) into a looped tab, referring to Creating a Looped Tab on page 6. Place the raw edges of the tab centered and under the bottom edge of the pocket even with the seam allowance and pin in place.

4. Stitch the pocket to the front of the scrubs top using two rows of stitching spaced ¼ inch apart.

Pleated Ruffles

1. Fold each 2-inch-wide ruffle strip in half, wrong sides together, and press. Align the raw edges of the strip along a measuring tape anchored to a table. Use a fabric marker to mark 1-inch increments on the strip (Figure 5).

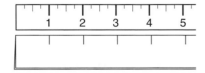

Figure 5

2. Starting from the left end of each strip, skip the first mark, fold the second mark to the third mark and pin. Fold the fourth mark to the fifth, continuing until you reach the end of the strip (Figure 6). Do not remove pins. Press.

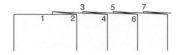

Figure 6

3. For each lower pocket, with right sides together, pin the raw edge of one pleated strip to the top of pocket. Release last pleat and trim length of strip to match pocket width (Figure 7).

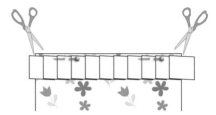

Figure 7

4. Stitch pleated strip to pocket top. Finish seam and short ends of pleated strip with overcast stitch. Press seam allowance toward pocket. Fold pocket side seam allowance and pleated strip to wrong side of pocket. Re-stitch the pocket to the scrubs top.

5. Cut two pieces of pleated strip the length of sleeve bottoms plus 1 inch. Unfold strip ends. With right sides together, stitch ends using a ½-inch seam. Press seam open (Figure 8).

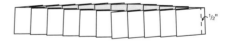

Figure 8

6. Refold strip and adjust width of pleats, if necessary, to achieve a balanced look. With right sides together, pin a pleated strip to the bottom edge of each sleeve, matching seam in pleated strip to underarm seam (Figure 9).

Figure 9

7. Stitch pleated strip to sleeve. Finish seam with an overcast stitch. Press seam toward sleeve.

Scrubs Pants

Preparing Garment

1. Remove stitching from the hemline of both pant legs. Place pins in side and inner leg seams 18 inches from leg bottoms to anchor seams, referring to Deconstructing a Garment on page 5.

2. Open the side and inner leg seams to pins. Remove cut threads from all seams. Gently press seam allowances flat.

Appliqués

1. Apply fusible web to wrong side of remaining gingham fabric. *Do not* remove paper backing.

2. Using patterns provided, trace flower and leaf designs onto the paper backing of fusible web as noted on patterns. Cut around each design, leaving at least ¼ inch on all sides. Fuse to wrong sides of appropriate fabric scraps, as indicated on patterns. Cut on traced lines to make appliqués: two large flowers, two small flowers, five flower petals, one tulip, five leaves, four flower centers and one flower pod. Remove paper backing.

3. Fuse fabric-scrap flowers and leaves to right side of gingham fabric, spacing at least ¼ inch apart. Cut around each flower and leaf, leaving ⅛-inch border of gingham fabric visible. Remove paper backing.

4. Arrange flowers and leaves on front of each pant leg, referring to Figure 10 and photo. Fuse to pant legs following the manufacturer's instructions.

5. Add detail and stems to flowers using the gel roller fabric pen. **Note:** *Refer to Gel Roller Fabric Pen on page 5 for useful tips on using the pen.* Heat-set, following the manufacturer's instructions.

Figure 10

Finishing

1. To make a grid design over the flowers, lay a ruler over the pants leg at a 45-degree angle to the hem edge. Using a water-soluble fabric marker, draw a line at this angle. Mark and draw lines parallel to the base line, spacing lines ½ inch apart.

2. Mark additional lines at desired angle to the original base line to create a grid. Refer to Figure 11 for line placement.

Figure 11

3. Stitch lines with contrasting thread that will be visible on both the pants and the appliqués.

4. Re-stitch the pant leg seams. Finish seams with an overcast stitch. Refold hems and stitch. ❖

Small Flower
Cut 2
1 pink
1 dark yellow

Large Flower
Cut 2
1 light pink
1 dark pink

Leaf
Cut 5 green

Flower Center
Cut 4, alternating colors for flowers

Flower Petal
Cut 5 pink

Flower Pod
Cut 1 green

Tulip
Cut 1 dark yellow

Spring Flowers
Templates
Actual Size

House of White Birches, Berne, Indiana 46711   Clotilde.com

Summer Silhouettes

Create a "cool" but bold look with black and white embellishments on a white scrubs top and hot pink scrubs pants. Adding a gusset to the pants legs adds further flare to this summer scrubs set.

Materials
- White scrubs top in your size
- Hot pink scrubs pants in your size
- 2 fat quarters:
    black-with-white print (A)
    coordinating black-with-white print (B)
- Black gel roller fabric pen
- Transfer paper
- Low-tack tape
- Basic sewing supplies and equipment

Scrubs Top

Preparing Garment

1. Remove chest pocket from scrubs top. Set aside.

2. Place a pin approximately 4 inches from neckline edge on shoulder seam to anchor the seam, referring to Deconstructing a Garment on page 5.

3. Open shoulder seams to pin.

4. Remove cut threads from all seams. Gently press all seam allowances flat.

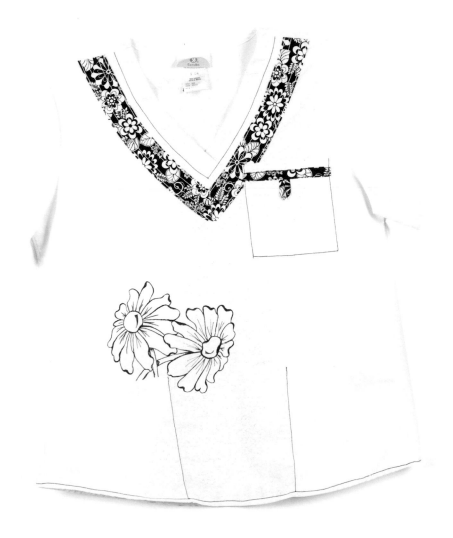

Cutting

Note: For cutting bias strips, refer to Bias Strips on page 6.

From fat quarter (A):
• Cut three 3-inch-wide bias strips.
• Cut one 1-inch-wide bias strip.

Assembly

V-Neck Trim

1. Join three 3-inch-wide bias strips together to make one long strip, referring to Bias Strips on page 6. Turn ¾ inch to wrong side along both long edges. Press.

2. Beginning at a shoulder seam, pin wrong side of bias strip to right side of scrubs top front about ½ inch from V-neckline. Fold bias strip at point of V-neckline (Figure 1), and continue pinning in place along opposite side. Trim bias even with shoulder seam.

Figure 1

3. Topstitch close to bias-strip edges using a decorative stitch and white thread, referring to Topstitching and Decorative Stitches on page 7. Sew two additional rows of topstitching spaced evenly between the bias-strip edges (Figure 2).

Figure 2

4. With black thread, stitch over original topstitching around original V-neckline banding.

5. Re-stitch shoulder seams. Finish seams with overcast stitch.

Upper Pocket

1. Turn ¼ inch to wrong side along both long edges of 1-inch-wide bias strip. Press. Using black thread, make a looped tab from a 4-inch length of the bias strip, referring to Creating a Looped Tab on page 6.

2. On the right side of the pocket, pin the looped tab approximately ¼ inch below the pocket hem (Figure 3a). Pin the wrong side of remaining 1-inch-wide bias strip to the right side of the pocket along the hem and covering the ends of the looped tab (Figure 3b). Topstitch close to both edges of the bias strip with black thread.

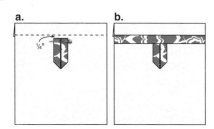

a.   b.

¼"

Figure 3

3. Turn original side and bottom seam allowances to wrong side of pocket and press. Place chest pocket in original position on scrubs top and pin. Using a decorative stitch and black thread, stitch the chest pocket to the scrubs top front.

Lower Pockets

1. Referring to Transferring a Design Pattern on page 7, transfer the flower designs (pages 32, 33) to the scrubs top above right-hand pocket (Figure 4).

Figure 4

2. Use the gel roller fabric pen to trace the transferred pattern lines. Add dimension by drawing lines thicker and thinner, adding shading and extra lines in petals. Use the project photo as a guide. Heat-set following the manufacturer's instructions.

3. Use a decorative stitch and black thread to stitch over hip pocket side seams and around scrubs top hemline.

Scrubs Pants

Preparing Garment

1. Remove hemline stitching from pants legs. Place pins in side and inner leg seams 18 inches from leg bottoms to anchor the seams, referring to Deconstructing a Garment on page 5.

2. Open side and inner leg seams to pins. Remove cut threads from all seams. Gently press all seams open.

3. Measure seam allowance. If necessary, adjust pattern seam allowance to correspond with garment seam allowance.

Cutting

From fat quarter B:
• Enlarge godet pattern (page 31) as indicated. Use enlarged pattern to cut two leg godets.

Assembly

1. Starting at bottom with right sides together, pin the leg gusset to the front side seam of one pants leg (Figure 5). Stitch. Finish seam with overcast stitch. Press seam toward pants leg.

Figure 5

2. Pin godet and front pant leg to back pants leg with right sides together (Figure 6).

Figure 6

3. Re-stitch pants side seam. Finish seam with overcast stitch. Press seam toward back pants leg. Using thread to match pants, sew two rows of topstitching close to godet edges (Figure 7).

Figure 7

4. Repeat steps 1–3 for second leg.

5. Transfer flower templates (pages 32, 33) to left pants leg following Transferring a Design Pattern instructions on page 7. Refer to Figure 8 and project photo for placement of flowers.

Figure 8

6. Mark transfer lines and add dimension to flowers following step 2 of Lower Pockets instructions.

7. Re-stitch pants inner leg seam. Finish seam with overcast stitch. Press seam toward back pants leg. Refold original hem in pants legs and re-stitch with thread to match pants. ❖

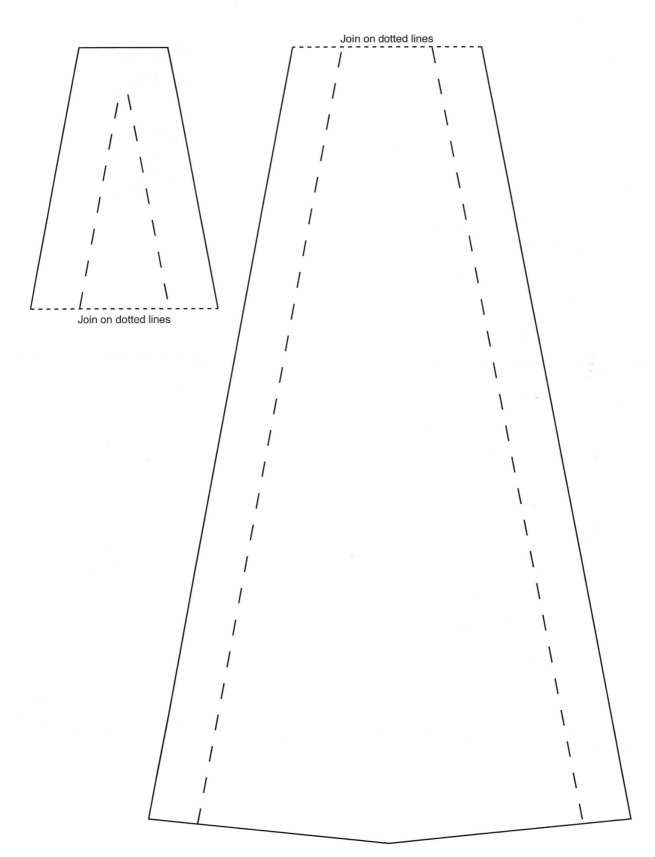

Join on dotted lines

Join on dotted lines

Summer Silhouettes
Leg Godet
Pattern

Summer Silhouettes
Template

Summer Silhouettes
Template

House of White Birches, Berne, Indiana 46711 Clotilde.com

Fall Leaves

Colorful fall fabric insets and topstitching create linear drama on a plain brown scrubs set. Add an extra-special touch to the pants with a removable pocket.

Materials

- Brown scrubs top with overlapping front in your size
- Brown drawstring scrubs pants in your size
- 44/45-inch wide fabric:
  - ½ yard brown leaf print
  - ¼ yard coordinating green leaf print
- Five ¾-inch buttons
- ¼ yard 1-inch-wide elastic
- ¼-inch-wide fusible web tape
- Basic sewing supplies and equipment

Scrubs Top

Preparing Garment

1. Place a pin 4 inches from neckline edge on shoulder seam to anchor the seam, referring to Deconstructing a Garment on page 5. Open shoulder seams to pin.

2. Along both side seams, place pins in seam 6 inches below underarm seam and 3 inches above hemline to anchor seams. Open both side seams between pins.

3. Place pins 4 inches down from pocket tops on inner seams to anchor. Open pocket seams from top to pins.

4. Mark neckline overlap on left side of front and remove stitching. Remove entire neckline band from scrubs top front.

5. Remove cut thread from all seams. Gently press all seams flat.

Cutting

From brown leaf print fabric:
- Cut three 2½ x 45-inch strips for neckline and sleeve bands.
- Cut one 1 x 4-inch strip for looped tab.
- Cut one 5 x 5-inch square for sleeve accents.
- Cut one 2 x 7½-inch rectangle for back elastic casing.

Assembly

Note: All topstitching should be done in complementary thread color.

Neckline Band

1. Fold each 2½ x 45-inch strip in half lengthwise, wrong sides together. Press. Being careful not to stretch the bias neckline, pin raw edges of strip to scrubs front neckline edge (Figure 1). Baste in place.

Figure 1

2. With right sides together, pin raw edges of neckline bands (that were earlier removed from garment) to neckline edge over bias strips. Stitch together using a ½-inch seam allowance. Finish seams with an overcast stitch. Press seams toward garment. Topstitch along folded edge of bias strip on short neckline band only.

3. On wrong side of top, overlap neckline edges at original overlap mark and pin at overlap and side seam (Figure 2).

Figure 2

4. Carefully turn top to right side; baste remaining raw edges of neckband in place so front lays flat. Topstitch along folded edge of bias strips on long neckline band, stitching through all thicknesses at overlap to secure.

5. Topstitch ⅛ inch from the folded edges of bias strips. Repeat, topstitching 3 rows along neckline banding, spacing ⅜ inch apart (Figure 3).

Figure 3

Lower Pockets

1. Sew three rows of topstitching ⅜ inch apart across pocket tops. Using 1 x 4-inch strip, make one looped tab following Creating a Looped Tab instructions on page 6.

2. Fold original pocket seam allowances to wrong side and pin pockets to scrubs top. Insert tab under left pocket inner seam at an angle (Figure 4) and pin.

3. Re-stitch pocket seams and any interior pocket seams, again referring to Figure 4.

Figure 4

4. With right sides together, re-stitch side seams, being sure to catch neckline band and pockets in seams. Finish seams with an overcast stitch. Stitch a decorative stitch over the scrubs top hem stitching.

Sleeves

1. Cut the 5 x 5-inch square across one diagonal (Figure 5). Fold under and press ½ inch on each short side of each triangle.

Figure 5

2. Fold sleeve in half and mark center of sleeve hem. Position and pin triangle, right side up, at center of sleeve with raw diagonal edge even with hem edge (Figure 6).

Figure 6

3. Edgestitch triangle in place close to folded edges. Repeat for second sleeve.

4. Cut two lengths from remaining 2½ x 45-inch strip the circumference of sleeve hem plus 1 inch. Fold ½ inch on both lengthwise edges toward center of folded strip (Figure 7).

Figure 7

5. For each strip, open flat and stitch short ends together using a ½-inch seam. Press seam open. Refold strip and press, and then open flat once more.

6. With right sides together, pin one raw edge of each strip to a sleeve hem bottom, matching sleeve underarm seam to strip seam. Stitch a ½-inch seam allowance along fold on strip (Figure 8).

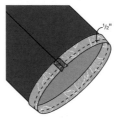

Figure 8

7. On each sleeve, press strip away from hem at stitching. Re-fold raw lengthwise edge of strip to wrong side of strip and then fold strip over hem to wrong side of sleeve along center fold. Pin through all layers. Hand–hem-stitch strip to wrong side of sleeve along seam line.

8. Topstitch ⅜ inch from triangle and sleeve band edge on each sleeve (Figure 9).

Figure 9

Back Waist Elastic

1. Turn ¼ inch to wrong side of all edges of 2 x 7½-inch rectangle for back waist elastic casing. Press.

2. Have intended wearer try the scrubs top on and mark the wearer's natural waistline at the center back. Position casing right side up centered over natural waistline and center back and pin (Figure 10).

Figure 10

House of White Birches, Berne, Indiana 46711   Clotilde.com

3. Edgestitch top and bottom of casing. Thread 5½-inch piece of elastic through casing, referring to Inserting Elastic Into Casings on page 6.

4. On each end of casing, stitch close edges through all layers, catching ends of elastic in stitching (Figure 11).

Figure 11

5. With right sides together, re-stitch original side seams of top and finish with overcast stitch. Topstitch over hemline.

Scrubs Pants

Preparing Garment

1. Remove stitching from hemline of both pants legs. Place pins in side and inner leg seams 18 inches up from leg bottoms to anchor seams, referring to Deconstructing a Garment on page 5.

2. Open side and inner leg seams to pins.

3. Measure seam allowances. If necessary, adjust leg gusset pattern seam allowances to correspond with garment seam allowances.

4. Remove cut threads from all seams. Gently press seam allowances flat.

Cutting

From brown leaf print fabric:
• Enlarge godet template on page 31 as indicated. Use enlarged template to cut 2 leg gussets.
• Cut one 1 x 6-inch strip for looped tabs.
• Cut one 7 x 27-inch rectangle for pocket bag.

From coordinating green leaf print fabric:
• Cut one 7 x 27-inch rectangle for pocket bag.

Assembly

Note: All topstitching should be done in complementary thread.

Leg Godets

1. Follow instructions for Creating a Looped Tab on page 6, to make two 3-inch looped tabs from the 1 x 6-inch brown leaf print fabric. Set aside.

2. Measure 6 inches from leg bottom on front side seam allowance and position a looped tab; cut edge even with pants leg edge (Figure 12). Baste to secure.

Figure 12

3. Starting at bottom with right sides together, pin the leg godet to the front side seam of one pants leg. Stitch using original seam allowance. Finish seam with overcast stitch. Press seam toward front pants leg.

4. Pin godet and front pants leg to back pants leg with right sides together. Re-stitch pants side seam. Finish seam with overcast stitch. Press seam toward back pants leg.

5. Sew a button to back pants leg corresponding to looped tab.

6. Cut 2½ x 2½-inch square on one diagonal making two triangles. Fold ¼ inch to wrong side on each side and press. Center and pin triangle at top of gusset, right side up. Edgestitch all sides of triangle (Figure 13). Repeat for second leg.

Figure 13

7. Press and pin original hem into pants legs. Re-stitch with matching thread.

Pocket Bag

1. Pin 7 x 27-inch brown leaf and green leaf print rectangles right sides together. Stitch a ½-inch seam on all sides, leaving a 3-inch opening on one long side. Turn right side out through opening. Fold opening edges to inside and press all edges.

2. On green leaf print fabric, mark fold lines at 11 inches (A), 19 inches (B) and 23½ inches (C) from top (Figure 14).

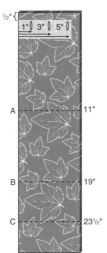

Figure 14

3. Mark buttonhole placement 1 inch, 3 inches and 5 inches from left side of rectangle and ½ inch down from top edge, again referring to Figure 14.

4. Fold up at A, down at B and up at C, referring to Figure 15, to create two pockets. Pin in place and press.

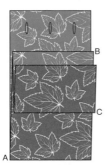

Figure 15

5. Topstitch close to outside edges and through all layers. Stitch again ⅜ inch from first row of stitching.

6. Center pocket bag over left side seam and mark button placement to match buttonholes, at lower edge of waistband.

7. Sew buttonholes in pocket bag top as marked. Sew buttons to pants where marked. Attach pocket bag to pants with buttons. ❖

Water-Bottle Cozy & ID Pouch

Show off your sewing skills with the energizing colors and soft cotton fabrics in this water-bottle cozy and matching pouch for keeping identification handy.

Materials
- 6 coordinating fat quarters
- 7-inch zipper
- ½ yard ¼-inch-wide elastic
- 26 x 20-inch rectangle cotton batting
- 1-liter water bottle with straight sides
- 2 large snaps
- 1 swivel clip
- Basic sewing supplies and equipment

Water-Bottle Cozy

Cutting
Set aside one fat quarter for backing.

From one fat quarter:
- Cut 3 (1 x 22-inch) strips.

From remaining four fat quarters:
- Cut 18 (22-inch-long) strips varying in widths from 1 to 2½ inches. *Note: Set aside remaining sections of fat quarters for ID pouch.*

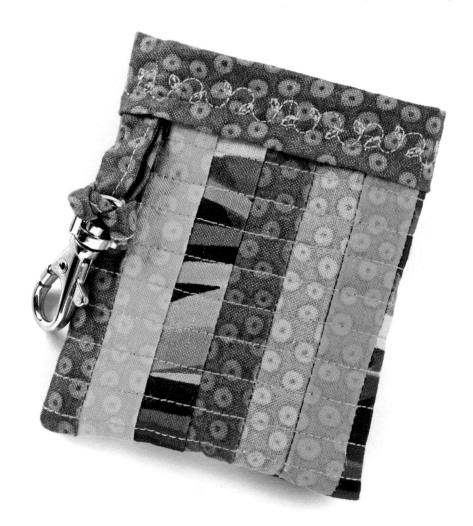

Assembly

Use ¼-inch seam allowances and sew right sides together unless otherwise stated. Press seams to one side, all in the same direction unless otherwise stated.

1. Arrange fat quarter strips on a flat surface, alternating colors and designs.

2. Stitch long edges of two varying-width strips together. Stitch a third strip to the second strip. Continue sewing strips together to form a rectangle at least 22 x 16 inches (Figure 1). ***Note:*** *Cut additional strips if necessary.*

Figure 1

3. Cut pieced rectangle in half diagonally (Figure 2).

Figure 2

4. Referring to Figure 3, sew a 1 x 22-inch strip between the two halves of the pieced rectangle. Press seams toward diagonal strip.

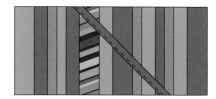

Figure 3

5. With the right side down, layer the fat quarter that was set aside for backing, then the cotton batting. Place the pieced rectangle right side up on the batting. Pin or hand-baste layers together.

6. Machine-quilt layers together, beginning ¼ inch from edge of diagonal strip and stitching lines ¼ inch apart on either side of the diagonal strip (Figure 4). Select a decorative stitch and sew down the center of the diagonal strip.

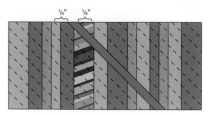

Figure 4

7. Measure and record the circumference of the water bottle, and its height from the lower edge of the cap to the bottle bottom. Add 2 inches to the circumference measurement; add 1 inch to the height measurement. Cut quilted fabric to these measurements, setting aside remaining quilted fabric for ID pouch.

8. Cut two pieces of ¼-inch-wide elastic the circumference of the bottle minus 1 inch. Set aside.

9. Trim two remaining 1 x 22-inch fabric strips to the bottle circumference measurement plus 1 inch. On each strip, press short ends under ½ inch. Using zigzag stitches, finish one long edge of each of the strips. Pin and stitch the unfinished edges of the strips to the long edges of the quilted fabric. Press strips away from the quilted piece.

10. Fold strips over raw edges to backing side of quilted fabric so finished edge on back falls just below stitching line. Pin in place. Stitch in the ditch to form an elastic casing.

11. Thread a piece of elastic through one casing, securing at ends with zigzag stitches. Trim 2 inches from second piece of elastic and thread through second casing to form bottom of bottle cozy.

12. Finish short raw edges of quilted piece with zigzag stitches. Fold each finished edge ½ inch to lining side and press.

13. Pin one folded edge to closed zipper tape, butting edge against zipper teeth with bottom of zipper at cozy bottom. Hand- or machine-stitch through all layers.

14. Partially open zipper and pin remaining folded edge to zipper tape. Beginning at bottom edge, hand- or machine-stitch through all layers, opening zipper completely to finish stitching. Reinforce bottom of zipper and cozy by bar-tacking bottom of cozy together.

ID Pouch

Cutting

From reserved quilted piece:
• Cut one 4 x 7-inch rectangle for pouch.

From leftover fat quarters:
• Cut one 5½ x 7-inch rectangle for pouch lining.
• Cut one 1 x 5-inch strip.

Assembly

Use ¼ inch seam allowances and sew right sides together unless otherwise stated.

1. Fold the 4 x 7-inch pouch rectangle in half, right sides together, to form a 3½ x 4-inch rectangle. Stitch across edges on one long side (opposite the fold) and one short side, leaving remaining side open. Turn right side out and press.

2. Fold the 5½ x 7-inch lining rectangle in half, right sides together, to form a 3½ x 5½-inch rectangle. Stitch in same manner as for pouch. Turn raw edges on open end ½ inch to wrong side and press. Turn under again ¾ inch from first fold and press to form a cuff.

3. Slip lining into pouch, wrong sides together, with lining cuff covering raw edges of pouch. Pin cuff close to fold through lining and pouch.

4. Press 1 x 5-inch strip in half lengthwise with wrong sides together. Open and press raw edges to center fold. Re-fold at center and press. Stitch along both folded edges.

5. Fold strip in half and insert fold into loop of swivel hook. Thread raw ends of strip through fabric fold and pull snug to secure strip to swivel hook. Pin raw ends of strip under lining cuff along side seam.

6. Topstitch around upper edge of pouch, securing cuff edge and attaching swivel clip. Sew snaps inside pouch for closing. ❖

Tech-Holder Armband

When you need to have your hands free and still keep something small close at hand—your cell phone, an iPod, identification card or a key—use this mini armband. It's great on the job and for your personal use.

Materials
- Scrap clear vinyl
- Scraps lime green and striped fabric
- One 1¼-inch D-ring
- One package 1¼-inch hook-and-loop self-adhesive tabs
- Basic sewing supplies and equipment

Cutting
From scrap vinyl:
- Cut one 3 x 3-inch square.

From lime green scraps:
- Cut one 1¾ x 18-inch strip.
- Cut one 3½ x 4¾-inch rectangle.

From striped fabric scraps
- Cut two 1 x 3-inch strips.
- Cut two 1½ x 3½-inch strips.
- Cut one 3½ x 4¾-inch rectangle.

Assembly
***Note:** Use ¼-inch seam allowances unless otherwise indicated.*

1. With right sides together, press 1¾ x 18-inch lime green strip in half. Trim one short end at an angle (Figure 1). Stitch together along length and angled short end. Turn right side out and press.

Figure 1

2. Apply seven loop tabs to strip beginning 4 inches from angled end and spaced ¾ inch apart (Figure 2).

Figure 2

3. Topstitch ⅛ inch from all sides of strip using a decorative stitch and sewing through loop tabs. Apply two hook tabs close to angled end of strip. Stitch through center of tabs (Figure 3).

Figure 3

4. Cut 2 inches from squared end of strip. Set aside remainder of strip. Thread 2-inch piece through D-ring. Match raw ends, pin together and stitch across strip close to D-ring (Figure 4). Set aside.

Figure 4

5. With right sides together, stitch the 1 x 3-inch strips to two opposite sides of vinyl square. Finger-press strips away from vinyl.

6. With right sides together, stitch one 1½ x 3½-inch strip to third side of vinyl square. Finger-press strip away from vinyl.

7. Press ¼ inch to wrong side of one lengthwise edge of second 1½ x 3½-inch strip. With right sides together, stitch raw edge of strip to fourth side of vinyl square. Wrap strip over vinyl edge to wrong side, enclosing top edge of vinyl.

8. Topstitch close to seam, catching folded edge of strip on wrong side (Figure 5).

Figure 5

9. Layer vinyl/striped fabric rectangle on 3½ x 4¾-inch striped fabric rectangle right sides up with bottom edges even. Center short armband piece with D-ring on left side of layers and long armband piece on right side with loop tabs facing down (Figure 6). Keep opposite ends of armband pieces away from seam allowances, again referring to Figure 6.

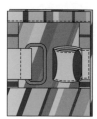

Figure 6

10. Layer lime green rectangle right side down, edges even with other rectangles. Pin to secure. Stitch all edges, leaving bottom open for turning. Turn right side out. Pull armband pieces to sides of tech holder. Fold raw edges of opening to inside. Press edges, keeping iron away from vinyl.

11. Topstitch close to all edges of tech holder, stitching bottom opening closed. ❖

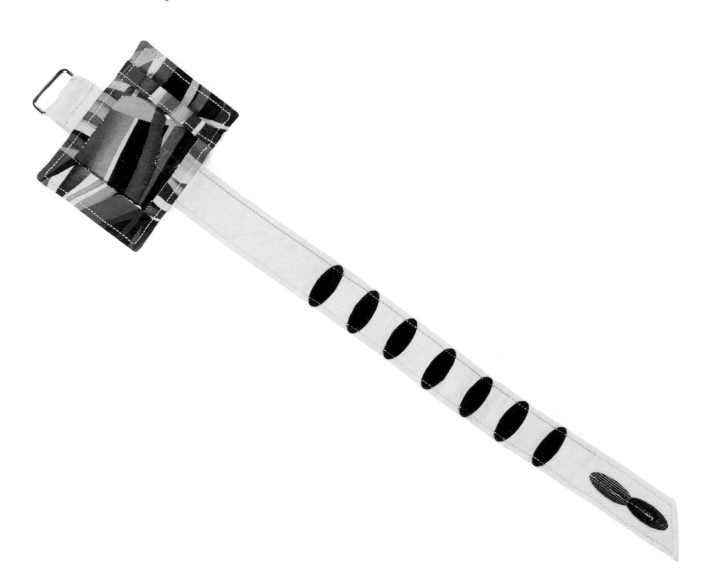

Metric Conversion Charts

Metric Conversions

yards	x	.9144	=	metres (m)
yards	x	91.44	=	centimetres (cm)
inches	x	2.54	=	centimetres (cm)
inches	x	25.40	=	millimetres (mm)
inches	x	.0254	=	metres (m)

centimetres	x	.3937	=	inches
metres	x	1.0936	=	yards

Standard Equivalents

⅛ inch	=	3.20mm	=	0.32cm
¼ inch	=	6.35mm	=	0.635cm
⅜ inch	=	9.50mm	=	0.95cm
½ inch	=	12.70mm	=	1.27cm
⅝ inch	=	15.90mm	=	1.59cm
¾ inch	=	19.10mm	=	1.91cm
⅞ inch	=	22.20mm	=	2.22cm
1 inch	=	25.40mm	=	2.54cm
⅛ yard	=	11.43cm	=	0.11m
¼ yard	=	22.86cm	=	0.23m
⅜ yard	=	34.29cm	=	0.34m
½ yard	=	45.72cm	=	0.46m
⅝ yard	=	57.15cm	=	0.57m
¾ yard	=	68.58cm	=	0.69m
⅞ yard	=	80.00cm	=	0.80m
1 yard	=	91.44cm	=	0.91m

1⅛ yards	=	102.87cm	=	1.03m
1¼ yards	=	114.30cm	=	1.14m
1⅜ yards	=	125.73cm	=	1.26m
1½ yards	=	137.16cm	=	1.37m
1⅝ yards	=	148.59cm	=	1.49m
1¾ yards	=	160.02cm	=	1.60m
1⅞ yards	=	171.44cm	=	1.71m
2 yards	=	182.88cm	=	1.83m
2⅛ yards	=	194.31cm	=	1.94m
2¼ yards	=	205.74cm	=	2.06m
2⅜ yards	=	217.17cm	=	2.17m
2½ yards	=	228.60cm	=	2.29m
2⅝ yards	=	240.03cm	=	2.40m
2¾ yards	=	251.46cm	=	2.51m
2⅞ yards	=	262.88cm	=	2.63m
3 yards	=	274.32cm	=	2.74m
3⅛ yards	=	285.75cm	=	2.86m
3¼ yards	=	297.18cm	=	2.97m
3⅜ yards	=	308.61cm	=	3.09m
3½ yards	=	320.04cm	=	3.20m
3⅝ yards	=	331.47cm	=	3.31m
3¾ yards	=	342.90cm	=	3.43m
3⅞ yards	=	354.32cm	=	3.54m
4 yards	=	365.76cm	=	3.66m
4⅛ yards	=	377.19cm	=	3.77m
4¼ yards	=	388.62cm	=	3.89m
4⅜ yards	=	400.05cm	=	4.00m
4½ yards	=	411.48cm	=	4.11m
4⅝ yards	=	422.91cm	=	4.23m
4¾ yards	=	434.34cm	=	4.34m
4⅞ yards	=	445.76cm	=	4.46m
5 yards	=	457.20cm	=	4.57m

E-mail: Customer_Service@whitebirches.com

HOUSE of WHITE BIRCHES
PUBLISHERS SINCE 1947

Scrubs & More is published by DRG, 306 East Parr Road, Berne, IN 46711, telephone (260) 589-4000. Printed in USA. Copyright © 2010 DRG. All rights reserved. This publication may not be reproduced in part or in whole without written permission from the publisher.

RETAIL STORES: If you would like to carry this pattern book or any other DRG publications, call the Wholesale Department at Annie's Attic to set up a direct account: (903) 636-4303. Also, request a complete listing of publications available from DRG.

Every effort has been made to ensure that the instructions in this pattern book are complete and accurate. We cannot, however, take responsibility for human error, typographical mistakes or variations in individual work.

STAFF

Editor: Jeanne Stauffer
Editorial Assistant: Kortney Barile
Technical Editors: Angie Buckles, Marla Laux
Technical Artist: Connie Rand
Copy Supervisor: Michelle Beck
Copy Editors: Mary O'Donnell, Susanna Tobias
Graphic Arts Supervisor: Ronda Bechinski

Graphic Artists: Glenda Chamberlain, Edith Teegarden
Art Director: Brad Snow
Assistant Art Director: Nick Pierce
Photography Supervisor: Tammy Christian
Photography: Matthew Owen
Photo Stylist: Tammy Steiner

ISBN: 978-1-59217-283-2

1 2 3 4 5 6 7 8 9

Photo Index

8

18

26

34

40

40

44